D0609461

FRACTION AND DECIMAL WORD PROBLEMS: NO PROBLEM!

MATH BUSTERS
WORD PROBLEMS

Rebecca Wingard-Nelson

NEED
MORE PRACTICE?
Free worksheets available at
http://www.enslow.com

E **Enslow Publishers, Inc.**
40 Industrial Road
Box 398
Berkeley Heights, NJ 07922
USA

http://www.enslow.com

Copyright © 2011 by Enslow Publishers, Inc.

All rights reserved.

No part of this book may be reproduced by any means
without the written permission of the publisher.

Library of Congress Cataloging-in-Publication Data

Wingard-Nelson, Rebecca.
 Fraction and decimal word problems : no problem! / Rebecca Wingard-Nelson.
   p. cm. — (Math busters word problems)
 Summary: "Presents a step-by-step guide to understanding word problems with fractions and decimals"— Provided
by publisher.
 Includes bibliographical references and index.
 ISBN 978-0-7660-3371-9
 1. Fractions—Juvenile literature. 2. Decimal fractions—Juvenile literature. 3. Word problems (Mathematics)—
Juvenile literature. I. Title.
 QA117.W557 2011
 513.2'65—dc22
                          2009037894

Printed in the United States of America

052010 Lake Book Manufacturing, Inc., Melrose Park, IL

10 9 8 7 6 5 4 3 2 1

To Our Readers: We have done our best to make sure all Internet Addresses in this book were active and appropriate
when we went to press. However, the author and the publisher have no control over and assume no liability for the
material available on those Internet sites or on other Web sites they may link to. Any comments or suggestions can be
sent by e-mail to comments@enslow.com or to the address on the back cover.

♻ Enslow Publishers, Inc., is committed to printing our books on recycled paper. The paper in every book contains
10% to 30% post-consumer waste (PCW). The cover board on the outside of each book contains 100% PCW. Our goal
is to do our part to help young people and the environment too!

Photo credits: Shutterstock, pp. 5, 9, 11, 12, 16, 18, 20, 23, 27, 29, 31, 33, 36, 39, 41, 43, 45, 46, 48, 51, 54, 58, 61;
© Comstock/PunchStock, pp. 7, 14, 35, 52, 57; © Corbis Corporation, p. 24.

Cover Photo: Shutterstock

Free worksheets are available for this book at http://www.enslow.com. Search on the *Math Busters Word Problems*
series name. The publisher will provide access to the worksheets for five years from the book's first publication date.

Contents

When you cut a birthday cake into eight pieces and then eat one (or two), you've just created the basis for a word problem. Math is everywhere; you just might not realize it all the time because math isn't always written as a math problem.

This book will help you understand how fractions, decimals, ratios, and percents are used in word problems. The step-by-step method can help students, parents, teachers, and tutors solve any word problems. The book can be read from beginning to end or used to review a specific topic.

? ? ? How do I start? What do I do if I get stuck?
What if the answer is wrong when I check it?
Word problems are hard for me! ? ? ?

Get Involved!

Solving mathematics problems is not a spectator sport. You can watch a swim meet. But for YOU to learn how to swim, YOU must get in the water. The same is true for math word problems. You have to practice solving the problems! You may watch how others solve them, but try to solve them for yourself, too.

Practice!

Even the most gifted athlete or musician will tell you that in order to play well, you must practice. The more you practice anything, the better and faster you become at it. The same principal applies to problem solving. Solve more problems, and you become better at solving problems. Homework problems and classwork are your practice.

Learning Means <u>Not</u> Already Knowing!

If you already know everything, there is nothing left to learn. Every mistake you make is a potential learning experience. When you understand a problem and get the right answer the first time, go for you! When you do NOT understand a problem but figure it out or you make a mistake and learn from it, AWESOME for you!

Questions, Questions!

Ask smart questions. Whoever is helping you will not know what you don't understand unless you tell them. You must ask a question before you can get an answer.

Ask questions early. Concepts in math build on each other. Knowing today's material is essential for understanding tomorrow's.

Don't Give Up!

Stuck on homework? There are many resources for homework help.
Check a textbook.
Ask someone who does understand.
Try looking up sources on the Internet (but don't get distracted).
Read this book!

Getting frustrated? Take a break.
Get a snack or a drink of water.
Move around to get your blood flowing.
Then come back and try again.

Stuck on a test? If you do get stuck on a problem, move on to the next one. Solve the problems you understand first. This way, you won't miss the problems you do understand because you were stuck on one you didn't. If you have time, go back and try the ones you skipped.

Wrong answer? Check the math. It could be a simple mistake. Try solving the problem another way! There are many problem-solving strategies, and there is usually more than one way to solve a problem. Don't give up. If you quit, you won't learn anything.

② Problem-Solving Steps

Solving math word problems can be broken down into four steps. You are more likely to get a correct answer and have less trouble finding it, when you follow these steps.

Problem-Solving Steps

Step 1: Understand the problem.
Step 2: Make a plan.
Step 3: Follow the plan.
Step 4: Review.

Step 1: Understand the problem.

Read the problem. Read the problem again. This may seem obvious, but this step may be the most important.

Ask yourself questions like:
Do I understand all of the words in the problem?
Can I restate the problem in my own words?
Will a picture or diagram help me understand the problem?
What does the problem ask me to find or show?
What information do I need to solve the problem? Do I have all of the information?

Underlining the important information can help you understand the problem. Read the problem as many times as it takes for you to have a clear sense of what happens in the problem and of what you are asked to find.

Step 2: Make a plan.

There are many ways to solve math problems. Choosing a good plan becomes easier as you solve more problems. Some plans you may choose are:

Make a list.

Guess and check.

Draw a picture.

Work backward.

Use logical reasoning.

Solve a simpler problem.

Use what you know.

Use a number line or graph.

Use a model.

Use a table.

Write an equation.

Use a proportion.

Step 3: Follow the plan.

Once you understand the problem and have decided how you want to solve it, you can carry out your plan. Use the plan you have chosen, but if it does not work, go back to step 2 and choose a different plan.

Step 4: Review.

Look back over the problem and your answer. Does the answer match the question? Does the answer make sense? Is it reasonable? Check the math. What plan worked or did not work? Reviewing what you have done on this problem will help you solve similar problems.

③ Fractions

A group of six friends went to an amusement park. Five of them rode on a hanging roller coaster. What fraction of the group rode the hanging roller coaster?

Step 1: Understand the problem.

Read the problem. Are there any words you do not understand? What does the word *fraction* mean?
A fraction describes part of a whole thing or part of a group. The bottom number (denominator) is the total number of equal parts. The top number (numerator) is the number of parts being talked about.

What does the problem ask you to find?
The fraction of the group that rode the hanging roller coaster.

What information do you need to solve the problem?
You need to know how many people are in the group and how many rode the roller coaster.

Do you have all of the information that you need? Is there extra information?
All of the information is given in the problem. There is no extra information.

Step 2: Make a plan.

This question asks for a fraction. You do not need to perform any operations. Use what you know about fractions and the given information to solve the problem.

Step 3: Follow the plan.

Five of the friends rode on the roller coaster. The numerator is 5.

There are six friends in the entire group. The denominator is 6.

$$\frac{5}{6}$$

Step 4: Review.

Does the answer match the question?
Yes. The problem asked for a fraction.

Does the answer make sense? **Yes.**

Is it reasonable? **Yes.**

Did the plan work for the problem? **Yes.**

? ? ? ? ? ? ? ? ?

The school cafeteria served chicken enchiladas for lunch. Chelsea ate 2/3 of an enchilada and Michelle ate 1/2 of an enchilada. Billy went back in line for more and ate 1 3/4 enchiladas.
List the students in order from who ate the least to who ate the most.

Step 1: Understand the problem.

Read the problem. Is there anything you do not understand?

What does the problem ask you to find?
A list of the students in order from who ate the least to who ate the most.

What information do you need to solve the problem? Is all of the information that you need in the question? Is there extra information?
You need to know how many enchiladas each person ate. The information is given in the question as a fractional amount for each student. There is no extra information.

Step 2: Make a plan.

This is a comparison question. There are no operations to perform. Compare the three fractions to put them in order. One way to compare fractions is to write each fraction with the same denominator.

··

Step 3: Follow the plan.

Chelsea ate 2/3 of an enchilada.
Michelle ate 1/2 of an enchilada.
Billy ate 1 3/4 enchiladas.

Before writing the fractions with the same denominators, you can tell who ate the most. Billy is the only one who ate more than one enchilada, so his is the last name on the list.

Compare the two remaining fractions, 2/3 and 1/2.

$$\frac{2}{3} = \frac{2 \times 2}{3 \times 2} = \frac{4}{6} \qquad\qquad \frac{1}{2} = \frac{1 \times 3}{2 \times 3} = \frac{3}{6}$$

4/6 is greater than 3/6, so 2/3 is greater than 1/2. Chelsea ate more than Michelle. From the student who ate the least to the student who ate the most, the list is:

Michelle, Chelsea, Billy

··

Step 4: Review.

Does the answer match the question?
Yes. The problem asked for a list of students.

Did the plan work for the problem? **Yes.**

Write the fractions in a list from least to greatest. Make sure you have listed each student with the correct fraction.

 1/2,   2/3,   1 3/4
Michelle, Chelsea, Billy   Correct.

Adding and Subtracting Like Fractions

On Gage's mp3 player, 1/3 of the songs are from his personal CD collection. Another 1/3 of the songs are from his sister's CD collection. What fraction of the songs on Gage's mp3 player are from both his and his sister's CDs?

Step 1: Understand the problem.

Read the problem. Is there anything you do not understand?

What does the problem ask you to find?
The fraction of songs on Gage's mp3 player that are from both his and his sister's CDs.

What information do you need to solve the problem? Is all of the information that you need in the question? Is there extra information?
You need to know what fraction of the songs are from Gage's CDs and what fraction are from his sister's CDs. The information is in the question. There is no extra information.

Step 2: Make a plan.

This problem gives you two fractions. It asks you to find the fraction that is the combination of the two. This is an addition problem. Let's draw a diagram to solve this problem.

Step 3: Follow the plan.

When you draw a diagram to help you solve a problem, it should be easy to draw and easy to understand.

Draw a diagram to represent all of the songs on the mp3 player. Let's use a rectangle. The songs from Gage's CD collection are 1/3 of the total. The songs from his sister's are 1/3 of the total.
Divide the diagram into thirds.

Shade one of the thirds to represent Gage's songs. Shade one of the thirds to represent his sister's songs. What fraction of the diagram is shaded? 2/3

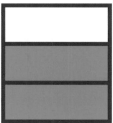

2/3 of the songs on Gage's mp3 player are from both his and his sister's CDs.

Step 4: Review.

Does the answer match the question?
Yes. The problem asked for a fraction.

Does the answer make sense? **Yes.**

Did the plan work for the problem?
Yes.

Is there another plan you could use?
Yes. You can write an equation.

$$\frac{1}{3} + \frac{1}{3} = \frac{2}{3}$$

To add or subtract like fractions (fractions with the same denominators), add or subtract the numerators and keep the same denominator.

Adding and Subtracting Unlike Fractions

Autumn and her girlfriends had a sleepover. They spent 6 1/2 hours watching movies. They spent 1 1/4 hours playing truth or dare. How much longer did they spend watching movies than playing truth or dare?

Step 1: Understand the problem.

Read the problem. Is there anything you do not understand?

What does the problem ask you to find?
How much longer the girls spent watching movies than they spent playing truth or dare.

What information do you need to solve the problem? Is all of the information that you need in the question? Is there extra information? **You need to know how long the girls spent on each activity. The information is in the question. There is no extra information.**

Step 2: Make a plan.

This problem asks for a difference between two amounts of time. *Difference* means subtraction. You can write a subtraction equation.

Step 3: Follow the plan.

To find a difference, subtract the smaller value from the larger value.

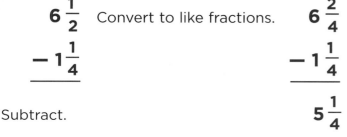

$$6\frac{1}{2}$$ Convert to like fractions. $$6\frac{2}{4}$$

$$-1\frac{1}{4}$$ $$-1\frac{1}{4}$$

Subtract. $$5\frac{1}{4}$$

The girls spent $5\frac{1}{4}$ more hours watching movies than they did playing truth or dare.

Step 4: Review.

Does the answer match the question?
Yes. The problem asked how much longer.

Check the subtraction using addition.

$$5\frac{1}{4} + 1\frac{1}{4} = 6\frac{2}{4} = 6\frac{1}{2}$$

Did the plan work for the problem? **Yes.**

To add or subtract unlike fractions (fractions with different denominators), convert them to like fractions first.

? ? ? Corey worked 36 hours last week at a restaurant. He worked 3/4 of those hours in the kitchen for $8.15 per hour. How many hours did Corey work in the kitchen? ? ? ?

Step 1: Understand the problem.

Read the problem. Is there anything you do not understand?

What does the problem ask you to find?
The number of hours Corey worked in the kitchen.

What information do you need to solve the problem? **The number of hours Corey worked and the fraction of the hours that he worked in the kitchen.**

Is there any extra information? **Yes. The problem tells you the amount Corey makes per hour.**

Step 2: Make a plan.

One way to solve this problem is to use a model. Corey worked 36 hours. You can represent each hour with a circle, or small item, such as a button or a penny.

Step 3: Follow the plan.

The denominator of a fraction tells you how many equal groups something is divided into. The denominator is 4. Divide the 36 hours into 4 equal groups. There are 9 in each group.

Corey worked 3 of the 4 groups of hours (3/4) in the kitchen. How many hours are in 3 of the groups? 27.

Corey worked 27 hours in the kitchen.

Step 4: Review.

Does the answer match the question?
Yes. The problem asked for a number of hours.

Did the plan work for the problem? **Yes.**

Is there another plan you can use to solve the problem? **Yes. The problem wants you to find 3/4 of 36 hours. The word *of* indicates that this is a multiplication problem. Multiply 3/4 × 36.**

$$\frac{3}{4} \times \frac{36}{1} = \frac{(3)(\overset{9}{\cancel{36}})}{(\cancel{4})(1)} = \frac{27}{1} = 27$$

To multiply any fractions, multiply the numerators and multiply the denominators. Reduce the answer to lowest terms.

? ? ? ? Dee is in charge of punch for a school dance. Each bowl of punch uses 1/2 cup of concentrate. How many bowls of punch will one gallon of concentrate make? ? ? ?

Step 1: Understand the problem.

Read the problem. Is there anything you do not understand?

What does the problem ask you to find?
How many bowls of punch one gallon of concentrate will make.

What information do you need to solve the problem? **You need to know how much concentrate is needed for each bowl of punch, how much concentrate you have, and how many cups are in a gallon.**

Does the problem give you all of the information? **No. You need to know that there are 16 cups in one gallon.**

Step 2: Make a plan.

This is a division problem. A gallon of concentrate is being divided into equal portions that are 1/2 cup each. Write a division equation.

Step 3: Follow the plan.

Write the problem using words first.

$\underline{\text{one gallon of concentrate}} \div \underline{\text{1/2 cup portions}} = \underline{\text{number of portions}}$

Change *one gallon* to *16 cups* so that the units match.

$\underline{\text{16 cups of concentrate}} \div \underline{\text{1/2 cup portions}} = \underline{\text{number of portions}}$

Now write and solve the equation.

16 ÷ 1/2 = 16 × 2/1 = 16 × 2 = 32
One gallon of concentrate will make 32 bowls of punch.

Reciprocals and Division

Reciprocals are two numbers that have a product of 1.
1/2 and 2/1 are reciprocals because 1/2 x 2/1 = 1.
You can find the reciprocal of any fraction by switching the numerator and denominator. The reciprocal of **3/5** is **5/3**.

To divide any number by a fraction, multiply by the reciprocal.
2/3 ÷ 4/5 is the same as 2/3 × 5/4.

Step 4: Review.

Does the answer match the question?
Yes. The problem asked how many bowls of punch.

Is there another plan you could use to solve the problem?
Yes. You could get one gallon of liquid and measure out 1/2 cup at a time, counting as you go.

⑨ Decimals

To earn an A in ninth grade, you must have an average of 93.0 or above. Garrett missed getting an A in English by sixteen hundredths of a point. Write *sixteen hundredths* as a decimal.

Step 1: Understand the problem.

Read the problem. Is there anything you do not understand? **What is a decimal? Decimals are numbers that use a decimal point to separate whole number values from fractional values.**

What does the problem ask you to find? **A decimal that has the same meaning as *sixteen hundredths*.**

What information do you need to solve the problem? **The numerical expression for *sixteen hundredths*.**

Is there any extra information? **Yes. You do not need to know the grade point average needed to earn an A.**

Decimal Place Value

Decimals follow the same place value pattern as whole number Each place has a value that is ten times the place on its right.

67.23

tens ones tenths hundredths

decimal
point

Step 2: Make a plan.

The problem asks for a decimal. Use what you know about decimals to write the answer.

Step 3: Follow the plan.

The word *hundredths* tells you that this decimal ends in the hundredths place, two places right of the decimal point.

The word *sixteen* tells you the digits to use are 16. Write the digits 16 so that the final digit (6) is in the hundredths place.

.16

There are no whole number parts. Write a zero as a placeholder in the ones place.

0.16

Sixteen hundredths as a decimal is 0.16.

Step 4: Review.

Does the answer match the question?
Yes. The problem asked for a decimal.

Did the plan work for the problem? **Yes.**

⑩ Fractions and Decimals

? ? Every day, Morgan and Steven walk 2 $\frac{3}{5}$ miles to school together. Write the distance as a decimal. ?

Step 1: Understand the problem.

Read the problem. Is there anything you do not understand?

What does the problem ask you to find?
The distance as a decimal.

What information do you need to solve the problem?
The distance as a fraction.

Fractions as Decimals

Fractions with denominators that are powers of ten are easy to write as decimals. For example, if the denominator is 10 (3/10), the numerator is written in the tenths place.

3/10 = 0.3

Fractions with other denominators can be written as decimals in two ways.

1. Write an equivalent fraction with a denominator that is a power of ten. 2/5 = 4/10 = 0.4
2. Use division. A fraction bar can be thought of as a division symbol. 2/5 = 2 ÷ 5 = 0.4

Step 2: Make a plan.

There is no operation in the problem. Write the fractional distance as a decimal distance.

Step 3: Follow the plan.

The whole number part (2) of the mixed fraction $2\,^3/_5$ stays the same. The fractional part ($^3/_5$) does not have a denominator that is a power of ten. Write the fraction $^3/_5$ as the equivalent fraction $^6/_{10}$. Change the equivalent fraction to a decimal.

2.6 miles

Step 4: Review.

Does the answer match the question?
Yes. The problem asked for a distance written as a decimal.

Did the plan work for the problem? **Yes.**

**Serge ran the 200-meter dash in 26.3 seconds.
Matthew ran the 200-meter dash in 26.16 seconds.
Who had a faster time?**

Step 1: Understand the problem.

Read the problem. Is there anything you do not understand?

What does the problem ask you to find?
The runner with the faster time.

Do you have all of the information you need to solve the problem?
**Yes. You know how long it took each runner to run the
200-meter dash.**

Step 2: Make a plan.

This problem asks you to compare two race times and find the
faster one. Compare the two decimals using place value.

Step 3: Follow the plan.

Write the two decimals in a column, lining up the decimal points.

$$26.3$$
$$26.16$$

The decimal 26.3 ends in the tenths place. The decimal 26.16
ends in the hundredths place. You can put a zero in the hundredths place so that each number ends in the same place.

$$26.30$$
$$26.16$$

Compare the digits from left to right. Both numbers have a 2 in the tens place. Both numbers have a 6 in the ones place.
In the tenths place, 3 is greater than 1, so 26.3 is greater than 26.16. Remember, you are looking for the FASTER time, or the lower number, 26.16.

Matthew had the faster time, 26.16 seconds.

Step 4: Review.

Does the answer match the question?
Yes. The problem asked for the runner with the faster time.

Did the plan work for the problem? **Yes.**

Adding and Subtracting Decimals

Mandi already has a pair of shoes for marching and is not renting an instrument. She needs all of the other items on the marching band fee list. What are her total fees for marching band?

Marching Band Fees:

Dress Uniform—$49.50
Summer Uniform—$22.25
Shoes—$40.00
Instrument Rental—$24.50
White Gloves—$2.25
Lyre—$3.75

Step 1: Understand the problem.

Read the problem. Is there anything you do not understand?

What does the problem ask you to find?
Mandi's total marching band fees.

What information do you need to solve the problem? **The fees that Mandi must pay.** Is all of the information that you need in the question? **Yes. The information is on the given fee list.**

Is there extra information? **No, but you need to know that Mandi does not need to pay for all of the items on the list.**

Step 2: Make a plan.

Use the list to find the individual amounts Mandi needs to pay. Add the amounts to find the total.

Step 3: Follow the plan.

Add all of the items on the list except the shoes fee and the instrument rental fee.

Dress Uniform	**$49.50**
Summer Uniform	**$22.25**
White Gloves	**$ 2.25**
Lyre	**+ $ 3.75**
	$77.75

Mandi's total fees for marching band are $77.75.

....

Step 4: Review.

Does the answer match the question?
Yes. The problem asked for a total dollar amount.

Check the answer.
Sometimes you can check your answer using a calculator.
If the problem is on homework or on a test, make sure you ask for permission first.

To add or subtract decimals, you can write the problem in a column. Line up the decimal points.

Remember to include the dollar sign and decimal point in answers that are money values.

⑬ Multiplying Decimals

?
?
?
The county pays $0.42 for each pound of recyclable paper that is collected from a county road. The freshman class collected 372 pounds of paper in a weekend fund-raiser. How much money did they earn?

Step 1: Understand the problem.

Read the problem. Is there anything you do not understand?

What does the problem ask you to find?
The amount of money the freshman class earned.

What information do you need to solve the problem? **How many pounds of recyclable paper were collected and how much is earned per pound.**

Is there extra information? **No, there is no extra information.**

Step 2: Make a plan.

The class earned $0.42 for each pound of recyclable paper. The words *for each* tell you this is a multiplication problem. Write a multiplication equation.

Step 3: Follow the plan.

Use words to tell what happens in the problem.

<u>372 pounds of paper</u> at <u>$0.42 per pound</u> = <u>money earned</u>

Replace the words with numbers and symbols. Do the multiplication.
372 × $0.42 = $156.24
The freshman class earned $156.24.

Step 4: Review.

Does the answer match the question?
Yes. The problem asked how much the freshman class earned.

Did the plan work for the problem? **Yes.**

Check your answer using estimation.
0.42 is a little less than 0.5, which is 1/2. How much is half of 372? 186. Since our answer, $156.24, is a little less than 186, it is a reasonable answer.

⑭ Dividing Decimals

? ? ? ? ?

A Green Club is earning money to plant trees. Each tree they plant will cost them $1.13. If they have earned $150, how many trees can they plant?

Step 1: Understand the problem.

Read the problem. Is there anything you do not understand?

What does the problem ask you to find?
The number of trees the club can plant.

Do you have all of the information you need to solve the problem?
Yes, you know how much the club has earned and how much it costs to plant one tree.

Step 2: Make a plan.

You know a total, and you know the amount one costs. This is a division problem. When dividing numbers that have several place values, you can make an educated guess, then check the guess using multiplication.

Step 3: Follow the plan.

Use what you know about decimals and powers of ten to make an educated guess.

If 1 tree costs $1.13, then 10 trees cost $11.30, and 100 trees cost $113.00. The club has earned $150.00, so it can buy more than 100 trees. Estimate that after buying 100 trees, there is a little less than $40.00 left, since 150 – 113 is a little less than 40. This is not enough to buy another 40 trees, but it may be enough to buy 30 more. Let's guess 130 trees.

130 trees × $1.13 = $146.90

To get your estimate closer to the exact answer, modify it using what you know. When the club plants 130 trees, it costs them $146.90. They still have $150.00 – $146.90 = $3.10. Two trees cost 2 x $1.13 = $2.26. Three trees cost $3.39. They can buy two trees more than the first guess, but not three. Check the modified guess of 132.

132 trees × $1.13 = $149.16

If they plant 132 trees for $149.16, there is some money left over, but not enough to buy another tree.

The Green Club can plant 132 trees.

Step 4: Review.

Check your answer using a division equation.

150 ÷ 1.13

1.13)150.00

```
          132
113 )15000
    - 113
      370
    - 339
      310
    - 226
       84
```

There is no need to continue. The club can plant 132 trees.
The answer is correct.

33

⑮ Ratios

Stu's phone records show that today he made 3 phone calls and sent 126 text messages. Write the ratio of calls to text messages in lowest terms.

Step 1: Understand the problem.

Read the problem. Is there anything you do not understand? What is a ratio? **Ratios are a way to compare two numbers using a colon, a fraction bar, or the word "to." "1 boy to 3 girls" is an example of a ratio.**

What does the problem ask you to find?
The ratio of calls to text messages.

Are there any special directions?
Yes. The ratio needs to be written in lowest terms.

What information do you need to solve the problem?
The number of calls made and the number of text messages sent.

Is all of the information that you need in the question? **Yes.**

Step 2: Make a plan.

The problem asks you to write a ratio. There are no computations needed to write the ratio.

Step 3: Follow the plan.

Use words first in the ratio, then replace the words with the values given in the problem.

calls : text messages

3 : 126

Ratios are reduced the same way fractions are. Find the greatest common factor of the two terms. The only common factor of 3 and 126 is 3. Divide each term by 3.

3 ÷ 3 : 126 ÷ 3

1 : 42

Step 4: Review.

Does the answer match the question?
Yes. The problem asks for a ratio.

Is there another way you could have answered the problem?
Yes. Ratios can be written in three different ways.

$1 : 42, \frac{1}{42}$, and "1 to 42" are all correct answers.

⑯ Rates

Juana's grandma lives 212 miles from her house. It took Juana 4 hours to drive from her house to her grandma's. What was Juana's average speed?

Step 1: Understand the problem.

Read the problem. Is there anything you do not understand?

What does the problem ask you to find?
Juana's average speed.

What information do you need to solve the problem? **How far she drove and how long it took.**

Is there any extra information? **No, there is no extra information.**

Rates and Unit Rates

Rates are ratios that compare two different kinds of quantities, such as time and distance, using the word *per* or a fraction bar. The units are included when writing a rate. For example, the rate $1.50 per 2 pounds or $1.50/2 pounds compares a cost to a weight. The units, dollars and pounds, are included.

When the second term in a rate is one unit, the rate is called a **unit rate.** Unit rates are found by dividing the first term by the second term. The unit rate for $1.50 per 2 pounds is $0.75 per pound, since $1.50 ÷ 2 = $0.75.

Step 2: Make a plan.

Speed is a rate that compares distance and time.
All rates are ratios. Write the ratio.

Step 3: Follow the plan.

The ratio of distance to time is 212 miles to 4 hours. Problems that asks for a rate, like speed, want the unit rate. Use division to find the unit rate.

212 miles ÷ 4 hours = 53 miles per hour

Juana's average speed was 53 miles per hour.

Step 4: Review.

Does the answer match the question?
Yes. The problem asked for the average speed.

Did the plan work for the problem? **Yes.**

Some rates have their own name.

Speed is a rate that compares distance and time, like miles per hour.

Mileage is a rate that compares distance and volume, like miles per gallon.

⑰ Distance, Rate, and Time

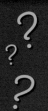

Dani swam the 500-yard freestyle at an average rate of 1.25 yards per second. How long did it take her to swim the 500 yards?

Step 1: Understand the problem.

Read the problem. Is there anything you do not understand?

What does the problem ask you to find?
The amount of time it took Dani to swim the 500-yard freestyle.

What information do you need to solve the problem?
The distance she swam and her speed.

Step 2: Make a plan.

The relationship between distance, rate, and time is given by a formula.
Use the formula to find the answer.

A formula is an equation that uses words or symbols to show a relationship.

For example, you can always multiply the length and width of a rectangle to find its area. The formula for the area of a rectangle is:

Area = length × width

or

A = lw

Step 3: Follow the plan.

The formula is distance = rate × time. Put the values you are given in the problem into the formula.

distance = rate × time

500 yards = 1.25 yards per second × time

500 = 1.25 × time

The missing value is one of the factors in a multiplication equation. Use the inverse operation, division, to find the missing value.

500 ÷ 1.25 = 400

The units used in the problem are the same in the answer. The speed was given in yards per second, so the answer is in seconds.

Dani swam 500 yards in 400 seconds.

Step 4: Review.

Does the answer match the question?
Yes. The problem asks for an amount of time.

Check your division by putting the answer back into the original multiplication equation.

500 yards = 1.25 yards per second × 400 seconds

500 = 1.25 × 400

500 = 500

Comparing Unit Rates

Nina's car uses a lot of oil. She usually buys one quart at a time for $2.79. She can buy the same oil in a five-quart container for $12.95. What is the unit price of the oil in the five-quart container? Which size container is a better bargain?

Step 1: Understand the problem.

Read the problem. Is there anything you do not understand? What is a unit price? **A unit price is a unit rate (see page 37) that tells the price of one measurement unit, like one quart.**

What does the problem ask you to find?
The unit price for the oil in the five-quart container and the size of the container that is a better bargain. There are two questions, so the solution should have two answers.

Do you have all of the information you need to solve the problem?
Yes. You know the price and size of each container of oil.

Step 2: Make a plan.

This is a two-part question. The unit price of the one-quart container is given in the problem. Use division to find the unit price of the five-quart container. Compare the unit prices to find the better bargain.

Step 3: Follow the plan.

Write the price of the five-quart container as a rate. Divide to find the unit price.

$12.95 per 5 quarts

$12.95 ÷ 5 quarts = $2.59 per quart

The unit price of the oil in the five-quart container is $2.59 per quart.

The second question compares the unit prices of the one-quart and five-quart containers. The one-quart container costs $2.79, so the unit price is $2.79 per quart.

$2.79 is more than $2.59.

The oil in the 5-quart container is the better bargain.

Step 4: Review.

Check your answer by finding the amount Nina would pay if she bought 5 of the one-quart containers.
Multiply the price of one quart of oil by 5 to find the amount Nina would pay if she purchased the oil one quart at a time.

$2.79 × 5 = $13.95

If Nina bought 5 one-quart containers, she would pay more than if she bought 1 five-quart container.

⑲ Proportions

Alisha knows that it takes her 18 minutes to drive to a town that is 8 miles away. She wants to drive to a town that is 12 miles away and thinks it should take about 27 minutes. Use a proportion to show whether her guess is reasonable.

Step 1: Understand the problem.

Read the problem. Is there anything you do not understand? What is a proportion? **A proportion is an equation that shows equivalent ratios.**

What does the problem ask you to find?
If Alisha's estimate of time is reasonable.

What information do you need to solve the problem?
The actual amount of time it takes Alisha to drive a given distance and her estimate of time for a different distance.

Is all of the information that you need in the question? **Yes.**

Step 2: Make a plan.

This problem tells you what plan to use. Some problems tell you the plan, such as draw a picture or use a table. This problem says to use a proportion. Proportions can be used in problems with two ratios.

Step 3: Follow the plan.

Proportions are usually written using fraction bars. Write the ratio of time to distance on each side of an equal sign.

$$\frac{\text{time}}{\text{distance}} = \frac{\text{time}}{\text{distance}}$$

$$\frac{18 \text{ minutes}}{8 \text{ miles}} = \frac{27 \text{ minutes}}{12 \text{ miles}}$$

Reduce each ratio to lowest terms.

$$\frac{18}{8} = \frac{27}{12}$$

$$\frac{9}{4} = \frac{9}{4}$$

Are the ratios equivalent, or very close? **Yes.**

The time Alisha estimates for the distance is reasonable, because it is in the same ratio as an actual time and distance she drives.

Step 4: Review.

Does the answer match the question?
Yes. The problem asks you to determine reasonableness.

Could you have done anything differently?
Yes. You could use cross multiplication to check the proportion.

$$\frac{18}{8} = \frac{27}{12}$$

$$(18 \times 12) = (8 \times 27)$$

$$216 = 216$$

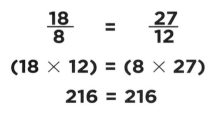

Owen can read 60 pages in 90 minutes. He needs to read another 156 pages for class tomorrow. How many minutes should it take him to read 156 more pages?

Step 1: Understand the problem.

Read the problem. Is there anything you do not understand?

What does the problem ask you to find?
The number of minutes it should take Owen to read 156 pages.

What information do you need to solve the problem?
The number of minutes it takes Owen to read a given number of pages.

Is all of the information that you need in the question? **Yes.**

Step 2: Make a plan.

Set up a proportion using the ratio of pages to minutes. Solve the proportion to find the missing number of minutes.

Step 3: Follow the plan.

Set up the proportion with a ratio of pages to minutes on each side of the proportion. Fill in the ratios with the numbers given in the problem.

$$\frac{\text{pages}}{\text{minutes}} = \frac{\text{pages}}{\text{minutes}}$$

$$\frac{60}{90} = \frac{156}{?}$$

One way to find a missing term in a proportion is to use cross multiplication. Cross multiply, then divide to find the missing term. Reducing the known ratio to lowest terms first gives you smaller, easier numbers for the multiplication and division.

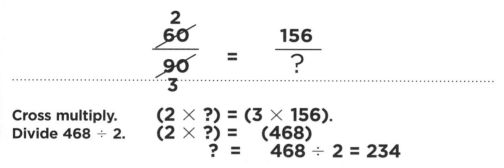

$$\frac{\cancel{60}^{\,2}}{\cancel{90}_{\,3}} = \frac{156}{?}$$

Cross multiply. (2 × ?) = (3 × 156).
Divide 468 ÷ 2. (2 × ?) = (468)
              ? = 468 ÷ 2 = 234

It should take Owen 234 minutes to read 156 pages.

Step 4: Review.

Does the answer match the question?
Yes. The problem asked for a time in minutes.

Check the answer. Write the proportion with the answer. Reduce both ratios to lowest terms. Are they equivalent?

$$\frac{60 \div 30}{90 \div 30} = \frac{156 \div 78}{234 \div 78} \qquad \frac{2}{3} = \frac{2}{3}$$

㉑ Scale Models

Alex is making scale models of a 60-foot-long ship and an 18-foot-long shark for a literature project. If his ship model is 20 inches long, what is the scale? How long should she make the model of the shark?

Step 1: Understand the problem.

Read the problem. Is there anything you do not understand? What is a scale?

A scale is a ratio that compares the measurements of a model or drawing to the actual item. A scale is often written using two different units in the same measurement system, such as inches and feet.

What does the problem ask you to find?

The scale of the model and the length that the model shark should be.

What information do you need to solve the problem?

The length of the real ship, the length of the model ship, and the length of the real shark.

Step 2: Make a plan.

Find the scale by writing the ratio of the model ship to the real ship and reducing it to lowest terms. Then use the scale in a proportion to find the correct length for the model shark.

Step 3: Follow the plan.

The ratio of the model ship to the actual ship is 20 inches to 60 feet. Both 20 and 60 are divisible by 20. In lowest terms, the ratio of the model ship to the actual ship is 1 inch to 3 feet.

A scale is written using an equal sign.
The scale for Alex's model is

1 inch = 3 feet

Write a proportion using the scale on one side and the known measurement for the shark on the other.

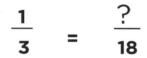

Some proportions can be solved using mental math. Think of the proportion as equivalent ratios. To change the bottom term from 3 to 18, you multiply by 6. Do the same thing to the top term, 1. Multiply: $1 \times 6 = 6$. The missing term is 6.

The model of the shark should be 6 inches long.

Step 4: Review.

How many questions were asked in the problem? **Two, the scale and the length of the model shark.**

Are both questions answered? **Yes.**

Read the problem again to be sure you have the correct units. **Yes. In this problem, the actual lengths of the ship and shark are in feet. The scale model lengths are in inches.**

㉒ Percents

? Julie works as a volunteer in equine therapy.
Eight out of ten people who work in animal-assisted
therapy are volunteers. What percent of the people
working in animal-assisted therapy are volunteers?

Step 1: Understand the problem.

Read the problem. Is there anything you do not understand?
What is equine therapy? **Equine therapy uses horses to provide therapy for mental, emotional, and physical disorders.** What does *percent* mean? ***Percent* literally means "per hundred."
Percents are ratios that have 100 as the second term.**

What does the problem ask you to find?
The percent of people working in animal-assisted therapy who are volunteers.

Do you have all of the information you need to solve the problem?
Yes. You know that eight out of ten people are volunteers.

Step 2: Make a plan.

You know the ratio, but need to write it as a percent. Rewrite the ratio with a second term of 100. Then write it as a percent.

Percents are written using a percent sign, %.

42% means

42 per hundred or $\frac{42}{100}$

Step 3: Follow the plan.

The ratio of volunteers to total people working is 8 to 10. Write an equivalent ratio with a second term of 100. To do this, multiply each term by 10.

8 to 10 = 8(10) to 10(10) = 80 to 100

Replace "to 100" with the percent sign.

80 to 100 = 80%

80% of the people working in animal-assisted therapy are volunteers.

Step 4: Review.

Does the answer match the question?
Yes. The problem asked for a percent.

In Jason's high school, 42% of the students ride a school bus home. What fraction of the students ride a school bus home?

Step 1: Understand the problem.

Read the problem. Is there anything you do not understand?

What does the problem ask you to find?
What fraction of the students ride a school bus home.

Is all of the information that you need in the question?
Yes. The problem gives you the percent of students who ride a school bus home.

Rewriting Percents

	27%	139%
As fractions:		
A percent is written as a fraction with a denominator of 100. The percentage, or number part of the percent, is the numerator.	$\frac{27}{100}$	$\frac{139}{100}$
As decimals:		
A percent is written as a decimal by dividing the numerator by the denominator (100). Simply drop the percent sign and move the decimal point two places left.	.27	1.39

Step 2: Make a plan.

Write the percent as a fraction. There are no operations.

....

Step 3: Follow the plan.

The percentage is the numerator part of a fraction with a denominator of 100.

$$\frac{42}{100}$$

Rewrite the fraction in lowest terms.

$$\frac{42 \div 2}{100 \div 2} = \frac{21}{50}$$

21/50 of the students at Jason's school ride the school bus home.

....

Step 4: Review.

Does the answer match the question?
Yes. The problem asked for the number of students who ride the bus home to be written as a fraction.

Check your math. Is the division correct where you reduced? **Yes.**

? ? ? ? ? ?

Sharelle found a jacket that originally cost $100.00. Today, there is a 40% off sale. How much will she save if she buys the jacket today?

Step 1: Understand the problem.

Read the problem. Is there anything you do not understand?

What does the problem ask you to find?
The amount she will save if she buys the jacket today.

Do you have all of the information you need to solve the problem?
Yes. You know the original price and the percent that is being taken off for today's sale.

Step 2: Make a plan.

Let's use a diagram to help solve this problem.

Step 3: Follow the plan.

Remember, a percent is a ratio out of 100. That means 100 is the whole, and the percent is part of the whole 100. In this problem, the whole is $100.00.

Draw a grid to represent the whole 100.

Shade 40 of the squares to represent the 40%, or 40 out of 100.

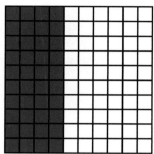

Since the jacket's original cost was $100.00, each square in the grid has a value of $1.00.

40 squares are shaded.
40 × $1.00 = $40.00.

Sharelle will save $40 if she buys the jacket today.

Step 4: Review.

Does the answer make sense? **Yes.**

Does the answer match the question?
Yes. The question asks how much she will save.

If the original price of the jacket was $200.00, what would be the value of each square in the grid?
There are 100 squares, so each would have a value of $2.00 (100 squares × $2.00 = $200.00).

How much would Sharelle save on a $200.00 jacket at 40% off?
40 squares × $2.00 = $80.00. She would save $80.00.

How much would Sharelle save on a $50.00 jacket at 40% off?
**Each square would have a value of $0.50 (100 squares × $0.50 = $50.00).
40 squares × $0.50 = $20.00. She would save $20.00.**

Mr. Morgan's last test had 25 problems. Each problem had the same value. Andy answered 22 of the problems correctly. What percent of the problems did Andy answer correctly?

Step 1: Understand the problem.

Read the problem. Is there anything you do not understand?

What does the problem ask you to find?
The percent of the problems that Andy answered correctly.

Do you have all of the information you need to solve the problem?
Yes. You know the number of problems and the number Andy answered correctly.

Step 2: Make a plan.

You are given the number of correct problems and the total number of problems. This can be written as a ratio of correct to total. Percent is also a ratio comparing a part to a total. Use a proportion to find the percent.

Step 3: Follow the plan.

Set up a proportion. Remember, a percent is a ratio with a second term of 100.

$$\frac{\textbf{percentage}}{\textbf{100}} = \frac{\textbf{correct problems}}{\textbf{total problems}}$$

$$\frac{?}{100} = \frac{22}{25}$$

Find the missing term using cross multiplication. Cross multiply, then divide to find the missing term. These ratios cannot be reduced any further before multiplication.

$$\frac{?}{100} = \frac{22}{25}$$

Cross multiply. $(? \times 25) = (100 \times 22)$
Divide 2200 ÷ 25. $(? \times 25) = (2200)$
$? = 2200 \div 25 = 88$

Write the answer as a percent.

Andy answered 88% of the problems correctly.

....

Step 4: Review.

Does the answer match the question?
Yes. The problem asked for a percent.

Is there another way you can solve this problem? **Yes. You know the ratio of correct answers to total answers. The fraction bar shows division. Divide 22 ÷ 25 = 0.88. Write the decimal answer as a percent by multiplying by 100 (moving the decimal point two places right). 0.88 = 88%**

The Percent Equation

In Jess's class, 75% of the students have camera phones. There are 284 students in her class. How many of the students have camera phones?

Step 1: Understand the problem.

Read the problem. Is there anything you do not understand?

What does the problem ask you to find?
The number of students in Jess's class who have camera phones.

Do you have all of the information you need to solve the problem?
Yes. You know how many students are in Jess's class and what percent of those student have camera phones.

Step 2: Make a plan.

Use the percent equation to find the number of students.

The Percent Equation

Percent problems relate three numbers: a whole, a percent, and a part. This statement relates the three numbers to each other.

Percent of whole is part.

50% of 10 is 5.

This statement can be written as an equation.
Of means you should multiply, and *is* means "equals."

percent × whole = part

50% × 10 = 5

Step 3: Follow the plan.

Write the percent equation.

<u>**percent**</u> × <u>**whole**</u> = <u>**part**</u>

Put the numbers you know from the problem in the equation. You know the percent and the total number of students, or whole. **75% × 284 = ____**

Write the percent as a decimal. **0.75 × 284 = ____**

Multiply. **0.75 × 284 = 213**

75% of 284 is 213

In Jess's class, 213 students have camera phones.

Step 4: Review.

Does your answer match the question?
Yes. The problem asked for a number of students.

Does your answer make sense?
Yes. 75% of 100 is 75. The number of students is a little less than 300.
3 × 75 = 225.
213 is a little less than 225, so the answer is reasonable.

Jared's computer has 500 GB of memory on its hard drive. The hard drive is 65% full. How much memory is unused on Jared's hard drive?

Step 1: Understand the problem.

Read the problem. Is there anything you do not understand?

What does the problem ask you to find?
The amount of memory that is unused on Jared's hard drive.

Do you have all of the information you need to solve the problem?
Yes. You know the total amount of memory on the hard drive, and you know what percent is used.

Step 2: Make a plan.

Let's use the percent equation.

Step 3: Follow the plan.

Write the percent equation.

percent × whole = part

Put the numbers you know from the problem in the equation. You know the percent and the amount of memory, or whole.

65% × 500 = _____

Write the percent as a decimal. **0.65 × 500 = _____**

Multiply. **0.65 × 500 = 325**

65% of 500 is 325

What did we find? 65% of the hard drive is full, so we found the amount of used space. You need to find the amount of unused space. The next step is to subtract.

500 − 325 = 175

There is 175 GB of unused memory on Jared's hard drive.

Step 4: Review.

Does your answer match the question?
Yes. The problem asked for the amount of unused memory.

Is there another way to solve the problem?
Yes. 100% is all of the memory, and 65% is used.
This means that 35% (100%− 65% = 35%) is unused.
Use 35% in the percent equation.

35% × 500 = _____

0.35 × 500 = 175 GB

> Always read a problem more than once while you are solving it. Make sure you are looking for what the question is asking for.

㉘ Tipping

When Ben and Singh eat out, they always leave a tip. Depending on the service, they leave 10%, 15%, or 20% of their bill. Tonight, they had Thai food, and the service was outstanding. They want to leave a 20% tip on an $85.00 bill. How much should they leave as a tip?

Step 1: Understand the problem.

Read the problem. Is there anything you do not understand?

What does the problem ask you to find?
The amount they should leave as a tip.

Do you have all of the information you need to solve the problem?
Yes. You know the total bill and the percent of the bill they want to leave.

Is there extra information?
Yes. You do not need to know that they sometimes leave different percentages in tips.

Step 2: Make a plan.

Problems that ask for percentages that are multiples of ten can often be solved using mental math. Use mental math.

Step 3: Follow the plan.

You can find 10% of a number by mentally moving the decimal point one place to the left.

10% of $85.00 is $8.50

20% is the same as 10% + 10%.

$8.50 + $8.50 = $17.00

A 20% tip on $85.00 is $17.00.

Ben and Singh should leave $17.00 as a tip.

Step 4: Review.

Does the answer match the question?
Yes. The problem asked for the amount they should tip if they want to leave a 20% tip.

Check the answer.
Use the percent equation to find 20% of $85.00.

20% × $85.00 = _____
0.20 × 85.00 = 17.00

Further Reading

Books

Abramson, Marcie F. *Painless Math Word Problems.* Hauppauge, N.Y.: Barron's Educational Series, 2001.

McKellar, Danica. *Math Doesn't Suck: How to Survive Middle School Math Without Losing Your Mind or Breaking a Nail.* New York: Hudson Street Press, 2007.

Sterling, Mary Jane. *Math Word Problems for Dummies.* Hoboken, N.J.: Wiley Publishing, Inc., 2007.

Internet Addresses

Banfill, J. *AAA Math.* "Fractions." © 2006.
    <http://www.aaamath.com/fra.html>

——. *AAA Math.* "Decimals." © 2006.
    <http://www.aaamath.com/dec.htm>

Math Playground. "Word Problems." 2008–2012.
    <http://mathplayground.com/wordproblems.html>

Index